Foreword

Electronic Commerce presents enormous potential opportunities for businesses and consumers. Its rapid implementation presents an urgent challenge for commerce, industry and governments within Europe.

Driven by the Internet revolution, Electronic Commerce is rapidly expanding and undergoing radical changes. Electronic Commerce is not some futuristic dream. It's the reality and is happening now, with many well-established success stories.

To ensure that European enterprises, particularly SMEs, will not lag behind in the rapid take-off of Electronic Commerce, the European Commission is stimulating a range of awareness creation activities aimed at increasing the use of Electronic Commerce.

Fortunately, each of the Member States of the European Union is well aware of the challenges presented by business technologies which are based on the electronic highway and that are reaching all corners of the world. In most Member States, public and private organizations are fully engaged in promoting the use of Electronic Commerce and making SMEs aware of the competitive advantages of its implementation in their businesses.

To offer further assistance to intermediaries who wish to inform SMEs of the business advantages of Electronic Commerce, the European Commission has published this guide of awareness creation initiatives. The information provided in this guide shows a large number of past and present, relevant initiatives within the field of Electronic Commerce that have been undertaken, not only in the Member States of the European Union, but also beyond Europe.

The aim of the guide is to help intermediaries find ideas for new initiatives whilst avoiding their re-inventing the wheel. This guide should, therefore, help intermediaries to improve the effectiveness of new and existing initiatives and increase the business opportunities for SMEs in the Member States of the European Union.

Rosalie Zobel
Head of Unit
DG XIII, Telecommunications,
Information Market and Exploitation
of Resarch
RTD: Information Technologies
European Commission

Livio Ricci Risso
Head of Unit: Distributive Trades
DG XXIII, Enterprise Policy,
DistributiveTrades, Tourism and
cooperatives
European Commission

Contents

Training & Research

Annexes

Introduction

Purpose of this guide

The purpose of this guide is to inform intermediaries - e.g. Chambers of Commerce, Euro Info Centres, branch organizations, etc. - of awareness creation initiatives in the field of Electronic Commerce. The guide has been compiled with the intention of evoking interest in the initiatives described and help intermediaries to set up new or adapted awareness creation initiatives for SMEs in their country.

Contents of this guide

The initiatives described in the first chapter all have a general orientation, aiming to create general understanding of the business advantages of Electronic Commerce and the technology required for implementing Electronic Commerce in an enterprise's business processes. The second chapter shows a number of general applications that can serve as a platform for executing business electronically.

The third chapter demonstrates how Electronic Commerce has already been applied in a number of specific industry sectors and European regions. The initiatives in the fourth chapter provide a selection of training and research projects that can be used as a source for new initiatives aimed at enhancing the knowledge-levels of Electronic Commerce among SMEs. A further selection of initiatives is provided in annex A.

How to find information in this guide

To assist you in finding information, the guide comprises a table of contents at the beginning and two indexes in annex B and C, at the back. Annex B lists the initiatives in order of country, annex C lists the initiatives in alphabetical order and shows the Web site for each initiative.

How to find information beyond this guide

As was mentioned both in the foreword and above, the aim of this guide is to evoke your interest in existing initiatives, and thus, assist you in setting up new initiatives in your region or country. To enable you to contact the organizations behind the initiatives described, considerable attention has been paid to providing up-to-date and complete contact details. Furthermore, the Web site addresses included for each initiative, which have been summarized in annex C, enable you to consult a wealth of information directly.

We kindly invite you to contact or consult any of the organizations mentioned in this guide, which hopefully will lead to an increased number of initiatives which will in turn, serve to further promote the use of Electronic Commerce among European SMEs.

GETTING
STARTED

Getting started in Electronic Commerce can, for many SMEs, be bewildering and confusing at first. What Electronic Commerce actually is, how it works, what it can do and the advantages it offers, can open up a whole new world. To help SMEs explore this world and to motivate them into seriously looking at its advantages, is a challenge that needs to be addressed by general awareness creation activities.

The initiatives described in this chapter provide general information, practical advice and clear guidelines - in the form of publications, demonstrations, or conferences and events - for incorporating electronic ways of doing business into an existing system. They range from general information on Electronic Commerce and examples of how to reach SMEs, to recommendations on building an effective Web site and hands-on demonstrations of the latest technology.

Name

Electronic Commerce and the European Union

Objectives

- Encourage the growth of Electronic Commerce in all Member States of the European Union
- Promote a favourable business environment
- Ensure access to the global marketplace
- Create a supporting legal framework

Target Group

Businesses and organizations interested in implementing Electronic Commerce

Approach

Web site offering information on all aspects of Electronic Commerce including:

- What is Electronic Commerce
- Who's who in Electronic Commerce
- The European Initiative in Electronic Commerce
- Reactions on the Initiative
- The G-8 Global Marketplace for SMEs
- Other policy papers of the European Commission
- Events and issues
- Projects

Description

The Web site offers a wealth of information that will serve as a starting point for anyone who is interested in business or policy aspects of Electronic Commerce. Links from the Web site lead to various policy papers, a discussion forum, related documents and information on initiatives in most Member States. A number of policy papers in each of the languages of the Member States can be downloaded.

Countries

Specific emphasis on the developments in Electronic Commerce in the Member States of the European Union. Follow-up of the developments in Electronic Commerce worldwide.

Results

This Web site has supported a large number of intermediaries in their activities to create and enhance awareness of Electronic Commerce.

Future developments

Continuous extension of Web site with up-to-date relevant information.

Partners

- European Commission, DG XIII, (Electronic Commerce and the European Union WWW-site)

Contact details

European Commission DG XIII:
Electronic Commerce and the European Union WWW-site

Fax	32 2 2968387
E-mail	ecommerce@www.ispo.cec.be
URL	http://www.ispo.cec.be/ecommerce

European Commission, DG XXIII
SME Policy and Electronic Commerce

Fax	32 2 2958984
E-mail	E-com@dg23.cec.be
URL	http://europa.eu.int/en/comm/dg23/index.htm

Name

DECLIC.NET

Objectives

DECLIC.NET's main objective is to achieve a maximum number of SMEs active in Electronic Commerce.

Target Group

All SMEs in the Lille region of France

Approach

- SME market as a while specific sectors : food, tourism,textile,electronics, health
- Flyers, reference brochures, business cases, seminars, workshops

Description

DECLIC.NET is a regional initiative, dedicated to Electronic Commerce. The initiative started in May 1998, and is carried by the Kalimedia Association for the first phase of one year.. After two years of awareness creation activities in the use of new technologies, DECLIC.NET now focuses on promoting the use of Electronic Commerce and moving from awareness to concrete use of Internet in the field of E-Commerce.

Schedule

Started 1 May1998. First phase of one year supported by KALIMEDIA

Countries

France: Regions of Lille and Nord pas de Calais

Results

Previous awareness campaign: Between 1 July 1995 and 30 September 1997, more than 500 participants from SMEs attended the KALIMEDIA seminars. A website with all the contents needed.

Partners

Chamber of Commerce, Regional Council, Conseil General, consultants, media

Contact details

KALIMEDIA, Michel Declunder	Tel	33 3 20288228
31, rue de la Fonderie	Fax	33 3 20363856
F-59200 Tourcoing	E-mail	michel@declic.net

Name

APTA - Austrian Platform for Telematics Applications

Objectives

- Stimulate the use of Electronic Commerce and telematics
- Coordinate and initiate telematics pilot and demo projects

Target group

SMEs, consumers, public and private organizations

Approach

- seminars
- exhibitions
- information days

Description

APTA officially represents the nine regional governments of Austria regarding all aspects of the Information Society, Telematics and Electronic Commerce. APTA serves as a network of competence and offers an overview of promotion activities that are undertaken in the deployment of the Information Society, it offers links to funding instruments, to ministries and to pilot projects in health care and education. APTA focuses its activities especially on SMEs.

Countries

Austria

Results

- Cooperation agreement with the Ministry of Science, Traffic and Art
- Members and partners in all Austrian provinces
- Partnership in EU projects (MIDAS, ESIS, et al)

Partners

Vorarlberger Telekommunikations-GmbH, Datenhighway Oberösterreich, Datenbahn Salzburg, INFO CONSULT Kärnten GmbH, Magistrat der Stadt Wien, Bnet, STE*KOM, ADV WIEN

Contact details

APTA Office
Lidmanskygasse 3/2
A-9010 Klagenfurt
Austria

E-mail infoconsult@carinthia.com
URL http://www.apta.co.at

Name

ECHANGEUR

Objectives

- Help European retailers discover, understand and adopt new technologies
- Enable European players in the retail industry to build appropriate strategies suited to the type of goods and services which are continually being modified by technological evolutions
- Assess the impact and issues generated by new technologies
- Facilitate and accelerate transition to Electronic Commerce

Target Group

European goods and services markets including SMEs

Approach

- Think-tank
- European training centre
- Demonstrations, seminars, newsletters, WWW based value-added information situated at the exhibition centre

Description

Echangeur is a large training centre and think-tank on technologies for commerce for the future. More than 150 demonstrations are on display and the latest technologies are shown to each visitor in a customized visit. Echangeur offers the following platforms:

- Store Tech: today's universe and tomorrow's store (front and back office, intranet/extranet, EDI, et al).
- Club membership privileged and customized access to Echangeur's services and products.
- Web Commerce: the technological revolution of the Internet for commerce (latest developments, Web merchant front and back office, new terminals, high speed web).
- Commerce Lab: future technologies such as virtual reality, Be OS, 3D.
- Web Analysis: ergonomics and usability studies on web merchant sites.
- Data Net: all the new technologies to optimize data use.
- Specials: commerce and technology news.
- Mini-Echangeur: a dedicated Echangeur workstation directly in the companies, with some of Echangeur's demonstrations.

Schedule

Set up in June1997

Countries

All European countries

Results

General awareness among retail players.

Future developments

Stay a permanent observation and demonstration centre on new technologies for commerce.

Partners

Paribas (Cetelem), LaSer - Groupe Galeries Lafayette (Cofinoga, Mag Info, e-LaSer), Informatica El Corte Inglés, Sears plc, Kaufhof Warenhaus AG, MSC (Multimedia Support Center), EIG Research Dyade, French Institute for research on Computer Science and Control (INRIA), Imperial College of London

Budget

Supported by the EU ESPRIT Programme
Budget at 7 MECU for 3 years

Contact details

ECHANGEUR
Groupement Européen d'Intérêt Economique
Parc technologique du Marais
66, rue des Archives
75003 Paris
France

Tel	33 1 44544130
Fax	33 1 44544143
E-mail	dbrouchet@echangeur.fr
URL	http://www.echangeur.fr

Name

Austria PRO (Austrian Electronic Commerce Association)

Objectives

Promote the use of EDI applications within the private sector and between public and private sectors.

Target Group

Private companies, traders' associations as well as national and provincial governments and legislative bodies, municipal administrations and all types of public authorities in Austria.

Approach

- Information and documentation on UN/EDIFACT standard messages, EDI software products available on the market, EDI users in Austrias
- Education (organizing EDI training seminars for beginners, UN/EDIFACT workshops, etc..
- Organization of campaigns aiming at the introduction of EDI and UN/EDIFACT in the public sector.
- Organization of sectoral interest groups consisting of AUSTRIAPRO members and their experts.
- Launching of pilot projects for EDI applications.
- Various services, such as maintenance of a pool of consulting firms offering special conditioins for EDI newcomwers, annual organization of an International EDI Symposium.

Schedule

Founded in 1989

Countries

Throughout Austria

Results

- Encouraging - EDI Implementation Workshop a very successful formula for step-by-step guidance to SMEs - significant interest generated within the European Community.
- Code of practice for larger organizations wishing to trade electronically with SMEs

Future developments

SMEs showing ability to use and 'do' EDI should raise the profile of the EDI user in the marketplace and promote EDI itself.

Contact details

Maria Ratzinger
AUSTRIAPRO, Austrian Chamber of Commerce
Wiedener Hauptstr. 63
1040 Vienna
Austria

Tel	43 1 50105 4313
Fax	43 1 50206 244
E-mail	ratzingm@aw.wk.or..at
URL	http://www.wk.or.at/austriapro

Name

Fabrimetal Roadshow

Objectives

Familiarize enterprises with the Internet

Target group

Managers of small and medium enterprises

Approach

A roadshow, with:

- Interactive sessions
- Talkhost
- Actors

Description

Two teams of five people toured Belgium with equipment and software. During 38 interactive sessions of 90 minutes, managers were introduced to practical demonstrations of commerce on the Internet. Two scenarios were presented:

- Internet based electronic purchasing
  This scenario demonstrated an inventory system and the stock transactions between two companies, a warehouse and a supplier.

- Internet enabled networking
  This scenario showed three companies forming a temporary, virtual company with all communications taking place via the Internet.

The talkhost talked the audience through these scenarios in a lively, entertaining and non-technical way, while three actors represented the companies.

Ample time was reserved for (lively) question and answer sessions whilst all technobabble, complicated jargon and hypertrendy theories were banned.

Schedule

Spring 1997

Countries

Belgium

Results

The initial target number of participants was 1.000 whereas the actual number of participants was 1.600. While the number of participants already using the Internet was 25%, after the shows participants indicated that within three weeks the number would be 75%. More than 60% of the participants evaluated the sessions as 'exceeding their expectations'.

All know-how, software, slides, scenarios, script and special hardware is easily transferable to any other Belgian or non-Belgian organization interested in pursuing the same goals of promoting the Internet, Electronic Commerce and networking to SMEs.

The national Belgian public TV broadcasting station BRTN has begun a series of programmes on the roadshows which is targeted at the same audience.

Future developments

Much more missionary work will be needed to convince Belgian enterprises to cooperate with complementary colleagues for the creation of 'virtual giants'.

More technicians will be needed for the installation and maintenance of all the small enterprise networks.

Partners

- Fabrimetal
- CRIF-WTCM
- Belgian Chambers of Commerce and Industry

Contact details

Karel Uyttendaele
Manager FABIT Information Technologies
Fabrimetal
Lakenweverstraat 21
B-1050 Brussels
Belgium

Tel	32 2 510 2542
Fax	32 2 510 2561
E-mail	karel.uyttendaele@fabrimetal.be
URL	http://www.innovation.be

Name

CEeC - Centre of Expertise in e-Commerce

Objectives

The Project has the following main objectives:

- facilitate the networking of e-Commerce experts and users in the Region;
- act as a conduit between the SME business community seeking innovation and those organizations providing EC support and technologies;
- provide independent personal guidance and on-going support to SMEs in determining requirements for EC innovation;
- provide opportunities for partnership between the Universities and SMEs through pilot projects;
- act as a catalyst for business change and economic development through EC.

Target Group

SMEs in the North-West of England

Approach

Direct, one-to-one assistance to SMEs and facilitating networking of experts and users across the region.

Description

CEeC is a network of specialists from business, educational, cultural and governmental organizations offering independent assistance to SMEs on e-Commerce as a means of improving their growth and competitiveness.

Schedule

The Centre was launched on 26 June 1998

Countries

UK

Results

The Centre has started to advise SMEs on e-Commerce issues and is currently developing the infrastructure of its network of experts.

Future developments

Expanding the activities of the Centre.

Partners

DATEL Advanced Systems Ltd., E-commerce Research Network, UMIST (University of Manchester Institute of Science and Technology), GEMISIS, Salford University, IRISI North West Partnership, Manchester City Art Galleries, Manchester City Council, Manchester Evening News, Manchester Federal School of Management and Business, MITRE and Manchester Technology Management Centre, Manchester Technology Management Centre, Millaer Seale, WebPromote Ltd., NettGain Solutions Ltd., NorthWest TechWeb, Royal Mail, Telematics Research and Applications Centre, Manchester Metropolitan University

Budget

The Centre has an annual budget of approximately GBP200 000

Contact Details

Tel	44 161 2003307
Fax	44 161 2003324
Email	info@Ceec
URL	http://www.ceec.org.uk

Name

DEMARCHE - Development of the Electronic MARketplace by CHambers of commerce in Europe

Objectives

Enhancing the capabilities of the European network of Chambers of Commerce to promote the effective use of electronic commerce in business

Target Group

- European enterprises (SMEs in particular) which have not yet been involved in electronic commerce
- Chambers of Commerce and Industry throughout Europe

Approach

- Publication of a brochure describing 15 best practice examples by Chambers of Commerce in Europe
- Transfer of knowledge and implementation scheme between 5 Lead and 25 Recipient Chambers of Commerce
- Final Conference to expose the project's results to a wider audience, and to plan future activities by the Chambers

Description

Many Chambers are providing electronic commerce training sessions, fairs and services to SMEs. DEMARCHE disseminates this know-how - held by individual Chambers - to as many European Chambers as possible. The final objective is more European SMEs being targeted by a larger number of Chambers providing more effective training and awareness campaigns.

Schedule

Start: 01/10/98 End: 31/12/98

Countries

France, Germany, Greece, Ireland, Italy, Portugal, Spain, Sweden, United Kingdom

Results

- 30 Chambers of Commerce around Europe promoting electronic commerce to SMEs more effectively
- Many more Chambers of Commerce in Europe focused on providing high quality electronic commerce support services to their member companies

Future developments

Eurochambres will continue to encourage exchange of best practice in electronic commerce between the 1200 Chambers of Commerce in Europe, in order to encourage more European SMEs to adopt new technologies as a tool to increase their competitiveness.

Partners

Eurochambres (coordinator)
Deutscher Industrie- und Handelstag - DIHT (Lead Chamber)
Infocamere Padova /IHK-GFI Dortmund (Lead Chamber)
Barcelona Chamber of Commerce (Lead Chamber)
Stockholm Chamber of Commerce (Lead Chamber)
South East Hampshire Chamber of Commerce (Lead Chamber)
Recipient Chambers of Commerce: Rhein-Neckar (D), Argolis (GR), Fthiotidos (GR), Thessaloniki (GR), Zakynthos (GR), Gipuzkoa (E), Madrid (E), Navarra (E), Ajaccio - Corse du Sud (F), Bordeaux (F), La Rochelle (F), Pays d'Auge (F), Quimper (F), Cork (IRL), Ireland (IRL), Wexford (IRL), Modena (I), Rome (I), Trieste (I), Vicenza (I), Portugal (P), East Sweden (S), Coventry & Warnickshire (UK), Glasgow (UK), Mid-Yorkshire (UK)

Budget

400.000 ECU, funded by Esprit

Contact details

Hylko Oosterloo
Eurochambres - Association of European Chambers of Commerce and Industry
5, rue Archimede, box 4
B-1000 Brussels
Tel 32 2 2820850
Fax 32 2 2300038
E-mail eurochambres@eurochambres.be
URL http://www.eurochambres.be

Name

GEMISIS 2000, The Virtual Chamber

Objectives

The overall objective of GEMISIS 2000 is to develop applications and services which use information and communication technologies (ICT) in order to assist with the social and economic regeneration of the North West of England.

The Virtual Chamber of Commerce project was created by GEMISIS with the objective of providing support and assistance to the SMEs of the North West to enable them to become more competitive both regionally and globally

Target Group

SMEs in the North West of England

Approach

The approach is bottom up, with a careful analysis of market trends and perceived needs of companies being used to design the initial sets of services. The project is seen as being the beta test phase leading to commercial roll-out and, as such, contains a significant element of evaluative research and feedback.

Description

Creation of an ATM based extranet with high bandwidth core available to SME subscribers offering a range of services including: websites, electronic shopping, secure transactions, business support and videoconferencing.

Schedule

Phase 1 commenced in June 1996 and is scheduled to finish in June 1999.

Results

100 companies on-line in Autumn '98, with an additional 400 by summer '99.

Future developments

In 1999 we intend to roll-out the service across the North West of England and into other selected areas of Europe. Generic elements of the service will be delivered as they stand and partnerships will be created in new areas to create content of local relevance. Discussions are already underway with partners in the Czech Republic and Malaysia to create similar services.

Countries

UK

Partners

University of Salford, Manchester Training and Enterprise Council, Manchester Chamber of Commerce and Industry, City of Salford, City of Manchester, Salford Royal Hospitals NHS Trust, ICL, Newbridge Networks

Budget

7 million pounds sterling, which includes a 2.5 million pound sterling grant from the European Regional Development Fund

Contact details

Keith Lawrence
Research & Graduate College
University of Salford
Salford M5 4WT, U.K.

Tel	44 161 2952909
Fax	44 161 2952900
E-mail	k.lawrence@grad.salford.ac.uk
URL	http://www.gemisis.co.uk

Name

Is Your Company Ready for Electronic Commerce and EDI?

Objectives

As an answer to the obvious demand for how-to-do manual on e-commerce, the Danish Chamber of Commerce has made a report (manual), that is particularly aimed at SMEs who wish to commence with e-commerce. It should be emphasized that this manual predominantly evaluates the business-to-business relationship and not so much business-to-consumer

Target group

SMEs

Approach

The manual contains three important issues in the matter of making the SMEs aware AND use e-commerce:

- It lists the most important parts of e-commerce that have an impact on any business that involves e-commerce. The four most important areas selected are:
  - the necessary change in business strategy;
  - the impact on the company organization;
  - the expected logistic gains;
  - the technology that is needed.
- It provides several best-practice examples from very different industries, which is recognized as the best way of engaging a business in any new form of business process. These examples have been selected in order to try and cope both with the different approach to e-commerce from the most common industries and also to show the different areas of e-commerce e.g. marketing, logistics, consumer sale etc.
- The manual contains an evaluation guide that enables the reader to evaluate his or her company's maturity concerning e-commerce. This guide goes through the four mentioned areas, strategy, organization, logistics and technology providing a how-to-do guide based on the evaluated maturity.

Description

The report (manual) can be acquired from any business in Denmark in three different formats: as a hard-copy manual, as a CD-ROM and finally on the Internet at the address: www.commerce.dk.

Countries

Denmark

Contact details

Det Danske Handelskammer

Klavs Steensen

Børsen, 1217 København K

Denmark

Tel	33 950500
Fax	33 325216
Email	klavs.steensen@commerce.dk
URL	http://www.commerce.dk/

Name

MIDAS - Multimedia Information Demonstration And Support Network

Objectives

To increase awareness and use of emerging multimedia information services and applications in Europe by providing practical advice to businesses and citizens

Target Group

SMEs

User groups in trade and industry

Citizens, through libraries

Approach

- Widespread geographical and sectoral coverage by way of local, support-based nodes which comprise a number of partner organizations. In total, 23 nodes in 18 countries with 108 organizations involved. These nodes also assist in making contact with other EU and national networks and initiatives.
- MIDAS-NET nodes communicate in the local language and are supported by a Central Support Team (CST) (link to cst@echo.lu) in Luxembourg. Common projects are also undertaken by groups of nodes for international information exchange and cooperation.
- All nodes have WWW sites with I*M Europe as the central link and umbrella supporter. This network of homogeneous sites disseminates information on EU initiatives, pan-European projects, multimedia-related activities within the European Commission, reports, studies and research results, and hosts communities for industry sectors.

Description

MIDAS-NET is an initiative of the INFO2000 programme of the EU designed to enable SMEs and citizens to understand opportunities and value of multimedia computers and networked communications. It seeks to address a lack of accessible practical information in respective languages that can address local business and individual needs.

Schedule

Operational since January 1997

Countries

Austria, Belgium, Denmark, Finland, France, Germany, Greece, Iceland, Ireland, Italy, Luxembourg, Netherlands, Norway, Portugal, Spain, Sweden, United Kingdom

Results

The first eighteen months have been very successful:

- Over 2500 people attending 15 kick-off events throughout Europe
- Political participation at ministerial level
- Many different events have already taken place and many more are planned in the 18 countries
- The network was the key promotional event in the EuroPrix MultiMediaArt 98
- A network of WWW servers showing high currency and interactivity
- Awareness projects are attracting widespread participation

Future developments

- More events planned in response to specific information requirements
- User groups in trade and industry being set up for demonstration of best practice purposes
- Extensive participation of MIDAS-NET with other EU initiatives (e.g. European Information Society Awareness Week, NetD@ys).

Partners

Collaboration with other European initiatives, e.g.: Multilingual Information Society programme (MLIS), NetD@ys, Innovation Relay Centres, BC-NET (Business Cooperation Network), Euro Info Centres, EUROGI, EUROMAP, BICs (Business Innovation Centres), PICs (Patent Information Centres), 4th Framework Program of Research & Technological Development (1994-1998)

Contact details

INFO 2000 Central Support Team
Ms Judith A. Pretty
BP 2373
L-1023 Luxembourg
Luxemburg

Tel	352 40 1162250
Fax	352 40 1162234
E-mail	cst@echo.lu
URL	http://www2.echo.lu/info2000/midas/home.html

Name

Memorandum of Understanding on Open Access to E-Commerce for SMEs

Objectives

To engage all sectors of industry in a consensus process of constructing a coherent and coordinated environment where both business and consumers benefit fully from the emerging electronic marketplace

Target Group

Major E-commerce system developers, banks, telecom operators, IT industries, service providers and users, in particular European SMEs.

Approach

The signatories to the Memorandum are associated to eight key groups according to their activity in the development of Electronic Commerce. Working groups are structured around the following key areas for cooperation: transaction billing, verification and confidentiality; interoperability of directories of small business services; exchange of legally binding documents and signatures; rights and liabilities.

Description

The Memorandum provides a framework for the major participants in development of electronic commerce to identify technical guidelines which can ensure interoperability and good practice guidelines to build confidence.

Schedule

Initiated in April 1996 and will continue to the end of 1998

Results

Good practice guidelines on coherence and interoperability in E-commerce

Partners

Over 110 organizations in the sectors of information and communication technologies, financial services, directory publishers, small business associations and regional economic and trade organizations

Contact details

Dr. J.J Kamp		Peter Johnston, European Commission
ABN-AMRO Bank, Brussels		DG XIII-B1, Office: BU-9 5/38
Tel	32 2 5460396	32 2 2963460
E-mail	jaap.kamp@abnamro.com	peter.johnston@postman.dg13.cec.be
URL	http://www.ispo.cec.be/ecommerce/mou/default.htm	

Name

Sp.OED

Objectives

Offer a central information service

Target group

Dutch enterprises

Approach

Information programmes, offering:

- Brochure
- Web site, which includes a newsletter and sample projects

Description

An information programme which helps to stimulate large-scale application of electronic highways. The project secretariat assists in seeking contacts with organizations or companies which carry out projects or develop applications related to the electronic highway. Visitors to the Web site can send in requests for advice and assistance via the electronic newsletter. This approach brings the demand and supply of services together. Practical examples displayed on the Web site provide insight into the new markets which are opening up on the electronic highway.

Countries

The Netherlands

Partners

- Ministry of Economic Affairs
- VNO-NCW
- MKB-Nederland

Contact details

Sp.OED-projectsecretariaat
Postbus 75537
1070 AM Amsterdam
The Netherlands

Tel	31 20 4874040
Fax	31 20 6697265
E-mail	spoed@wirehub.net
URL	http://spoed.wirehub.net

Name

KITE - Knowledge and Information Transfer on Electronic Commerce

Objectives

- Increase knowledge, understanding and awareness regarding electronic commerce in targeted sectors of SMEs.
- Create understanding and knowledge of electronic commerce with intermediaries.
- Facilitate the transfer of knowledge between institutions and organizations active in developing electronic commerce projects and trials.
- Accelerate the development of best practice in electronic commerce and increase opportunities for commercial exploitation.

Target Group

Intermediaries of SMEs and institutions such as:

- chambers of commerce
- regional development bodies
- trade associations
- innovation relay centres
- legal and professional service providers
- telecommunications suppliers
- banks and other financial service providers.

Approach

- Support activities with the aim to close the gap between electronic commerce policy and its practical implementation in European SMEs, in particular the centres of competence.
- Create understanding on electronic commerce with intermediaries, e.g.: provide banks with knowledge on electronic commerce
- Judge credit requests for business projects and provide business organizations such as chambers of commerce, trade associations, innovation relay centres with concise, high quality but easy to understand information to give guidance to their clients.
- Contribute to the analysis of policies on electronic commerce.
- Produce a worldwide inventory on electronic commerce initiatives (>250 entries) and a worldwide guide of best practice in electronic commerce (>100 entries).
- Provide logistical and organizational support to the G8 pilot project "A Global Marketplace for SMEs" and expert participation in the steering committee meetings; publish and disseminate results of the G8 pilot project activities, specifically focusing on best practice.

Description

- Worldwide inventory and best practice guide on electronic commerce initiatives
- Support of G8 pilot project "A Global Marketplace for SMEs"

Schedule

June 1998 to January 2000

Countries

Worldwide scope of activities

Results

- Increased knowledge, understanding and awareness regarding electronic commerce among intermediaries.
- Worldwide inventory of initiatives in electronic commerce (>250 entries)
- Worldwide guide of best practice in electronic commerce (>100 entries)
- Five newsletters
- Support of the G8 pilot project "A Global Marketplace for SMEs", elaboration of a final report on the activities of the G8 pilot project
- Strategy paper on creation of public awareness on electronic commerce.

Partners

- Teleport Sachsen-Anhalt GmbH (Germany)
- Martech International SA (Belgium)
- The Trefoyle Partnership (UK)

Contact details

Teleport Sachsen-Anhalt GmbH
Mr Uwe Leicht
Steinfeldstrasse3
D-39179 Barleben
Germany

Tel	49 39203 82030
Fax	49 39203 82031
E-mail	leicht@tsa.de
URL	http://kite.tsa.de/

Name

Media Plaza

Objectives

Accelerate the use of Internet and Electronic Commerce by demonstrating business applications of Internet, Extranet and Intranet.

Target group

Business managers and decision makers in the Netherlands.

Approach

A demonstration centre providing:

- Presentations on relevant themes of particular fields of business
- Tailor-made programmes
- Practical applications

Description

Media Plaza offers a four-hour programme during which a large number of state-of-the-art functions of the Electronic Highway are demonstrated. Each programme is preceded by an intake session to assess the knowledge level of Internet and the areas of interest of the participants. This information is used to determine the contents of the programme.

A session begins with an hour of audio-visual presentations which show the influence of the development of media and technologies such as Internet, Extranet and Intranet on business processes. Session are concluded with an evaluation in the Media Plaza bar. All participants are given a toolkit which includes a CD-ROM and a summary of all presentations.

In addition to this programme, Media Plaza can offer assistance, through its partners, in developing further activities around relevant themes or particular fields of business.

Schedule

Three years starting from 21 May 1997

Countries

The Netherlands

Future developments

Promote sectors on the Electronic Highway and cooperate with other initiatives

Partners

70 companies, of which the largest are:

- Jaarbeurs Utrecht
- Ministry of Economic Affairs
- ING Group
- PTT Telecom

Contact details

Media Plaza
Jaarbeursplein, hal 6
Postbus 30640
3503 AJ Utrecht
The Netherlands

Tel	31 30 291 41 11
Fax	31 30 291 41 44
E-mail	info@mediaplaza.nl
URL	http://www.mediaplaza.nl

Name

WeCAN

Objectives

WeCAN

- analyses the current problems of European Awareness initiatives in the field of Electronic commerce,
- develops and evaluates best practice awareness models,
- gives the models to professional organizers of awareness campaigns in Europe,
- motivates and supports organizers to implement the models in ongoing or future activities to improve their effectiveness and to make them more successful,
- creates synergies between different organizers and initiatives, thus enhancing the network of excellence over Europe
- helps to save money for European SMEs, awareness companies, eCommerce providers, and public authorities
- helps to make SMEs faster and more successful in implementing eCommerce solutions to improve their competitiveness in global markets

Target Group

The main target group are the organizers of awareness activities in Electronic Commerce. WeCAN will also provide benefits to the European Industry dealing with Electronic Commerce, Public Authorities and SMEs.

Description

WeCAN will serve as a platform for any initiatives dealing with eCommerce Awareness Creation in Europe. At the beginning of 1999, WeCAN will set the basis for a major European eCommerce Awareness campaign focused on SMEs supported by the European Industry and allying all current forces. WeCAN is registered as a G8 Test-bed.

Schedule

Start: 1 August 1998

End: 31.July 1999

Countries

EU member states, CEEC and Mediterranean -Countries

Results

- Best Practice Awareness Models in Electronic Commerce
- Plan for a Major Awareness Campaign in eCommerce in 1999
- European wide Network of Excellence in Awareness Creation

Partners

Austria: OÖ Datenhighway Entwicklungs-GmbH (ODE) (Project Management); France: Paris Chamber of Commerce and Industry; Germany: DIHT Deutscher Industrie- und Handelstag; Greece: Research Center, Athens University of Economics & Business (RC-AUEB); Italy: CE Consulting s.r.l.; Spain: CETEMMSA; The Netherlands: EDIFORUM; UK: Electronic Commerce Innovation Centre, University of Wales, Cardiff

Budget

1 Mio. ECU for Project

Contact details

OÖ Datenhighway Entwicklungs-GmbH (ODE)
Christian H. Leeb (Project Manager)
Jürgen Habichler (Project Management)
Hauptstraße 4
4040 Linz
Austria

Tel	43 732 712010-0
Fax	43 732 712010-12
E-mail	office@wecan-eu.at
URL	http://www.wecan-eu.at

GENERAL
APPLICATIONS

The general applications described in this chapter show what is possible in Electronic Commerce. Ready access to a wide array of information and marketing networks, which is brought within the reach of Small and Medium-sized Enterprises by Electronic Commerce, will significantly increase their competitive strength.

The initiatives in this chapter focus on the general provision of electronic trading platforms for businesses wishing to be listed and visible on the Internet and/or wanting to set up their own electronic trading and payment systems. At the heart of these initiatives is the provision of facilities for direct participation at a local, regional or national level, the ensuring of adequate standards and security measures, and for educational back-up and support.

Name

Grenoble Network Initiative (GNI)

Objectives

- Provision of range of professional services for SMEs
- Encourage new businesses

Target group

Small and Medium Enterprises

Approach

A 3 phase project consisting of:

- Set-up
- Sectorial services set-up, education & training, market research
- Preparation of commercial regulations, continued encouragement of new applications, education and training

Description

The GNI Work Group promotes an economical and consistent approach to Electronic Commerce and EDI in basic and sectorial services. To join the GNI, an enterprise must be based in, or do business with, the Grenoble area. Membership fee varies between 2500 - 7500 FF.

Schedule

To be run over a period of three to four years

Countries

France - the Grenoble region

Results

Projected to attain within 4 years: 1000 SMEs, 100 education and training units, 30 new services providers

Budget

$4 million over 3 years, sponsors and SME contributions.

Contact details

Grenoble Network Initiative
c/o INRIA
Joanna Payart
ZIRST - 655 Avenue de l'Europe
38330 Monbonnat, France

Tel 33 04 76 615356
E-mail joanna.payart@gni.fr
URL www.gni.fr/GNI/index.html

Name

South Wales Virtual Business Community

Objectives

Supporting SMEs in adopting certain key Electronic Commerce technologies

Target Group

South Wales manufacturing SMEs

Approach

A Pilot project using a test group of 15 South Wales businesses to trial suitable Electronic Commerce products and services

Description

This project results from the European Regional Development Fund having deemed South Wales an economically underdeveloped region. The area's manufacturing base has been targeted to evaluate the impact which electronic commerce services and products can have on the SME community and evaluate its support of different trading scenarios. The companies chosen are indicative of the South Wales industrial base - 13 are manufacturers, 2 are in the transport and service sector.

Schedule

Start: August 1996 and to be run for 24 months.

Countries

United Kingdom

Partners

- Welsh Office of the European Regional Development Fund
- Electronic Commerce Innovation Centre

Budget

Funding provided by the European Regional Development Fund

Contact details

Prof. Tony Davies or Martin Parfett	Tel	44 1222 876746
EC Innovation Centre	Fax	44 1222 874301
University of Wales	E-mail	ecic@cardiff.ac.uk
Cardiff	URL	http://www.cf.ac.uk/
United Kingdom		uwcc/masts/ecic/swec/

Name

SMARTS - SME and Regional Telecom Support

Objectives

The strategic objective of SMARTS is to increase the participation of Small and Medium sized Enterprises (SMEs) in the work and exploitation of results from ACTS. Participation in the framework of this project is defined as:

- full partnership or subcontructor in a new or established ACTS project;
- triggered usage of broadband technologies (including link services) in their own proprietary technology base;
- attendance at ACTS events;
- use of broadband technology products and services by non-technically based SMEs;
- engineers and scientists from SMEs joining ACTS projects and trials as guest researchers.

Target Group

Small and Medium-sized Enterprises all over Europe, which want to improve their production efficiency and business competitiveness by using advanced communications technologies and services

Approach

The project adopts three strategies aimed at lowering the barriers of remoteness, poor infrastructure and inability to fund the overhead of direct partnership in an ACTS project by:

- organizing a „Participation Broker" based on advanced communications technologies and services driven by the needs of SMEs offering services via a European network, which access points also in Central and Eastern European countries;
- performing a News and Information Service on topics and items related to ACTS and advanced communications which is of interest especially to SMEs who want to participate in ACTS; previous experience in this type of activities has been gained in the Telework Stimulation Action;
- actively promoting the participation of SMEs in the work to ACTS by increasing awareness among SMEs regarding opportunities offered in advanced communications, by brokering consortia with SME participation and by offering on-line SME support services to ease their burden and overhead of participation

Description

SMARTS is an initiative helping Small and Medium- sized Enterprises to acquire advanced communication services and implement them in their business procedures and work environment

Schedule

Duration: 36 month

Start of the project: January 1996

End of the project: DEcember 1998

Countries

A, B, BUL, G, E, F, FIN, GR, I, IRL, RUS, UK

Partners

Austria Technologie und Standortagentur Salzburg Gmbh;

Belgium European Business Network;

Bulgaria Association Regional Scientific Unions with the House of Science and Technology Plovdiv Acting through Marketing Invest Consult Plovdiv Ltd;

Germany Teleport Sachsen- Anhalt Gmbh, Ponton European Media Art Lab Gbr, Technologie Centrum Chemnitz Gmbh;

Spain (Espania) Parque Tecnologico De Galicia; France Cote D Azur Developement, Cicom Organization Sarl;

Finland Otaniemi Science Park Ltd;

Greece National Centre For Scientific Research Demokritos;

Italy University Of Trento;

Ireland North West Labs Ltd;

Russia St Petersburg Electrotechnical University Moscow, State University Redlab;

United Kingdom Wordbank Ltd

Contact details

Project Management: Cornelia Muhl
Teleport Sachsen-Anhalt GmbH
Steinfeldstr. 3
D-39179 Magdeburg-Barleben
Germany

Tel	49 39 203 820 30
Fax	49 39 203 820 31
E-mail	info@smarts.org

SMARTS Project Office:
Boulevard Clovis 39
B-1000 Brussels
Belgium

Tel	32 2 2854621
Fax	32 2 2306929
URL	www.smarts.org
	www.smarts.de

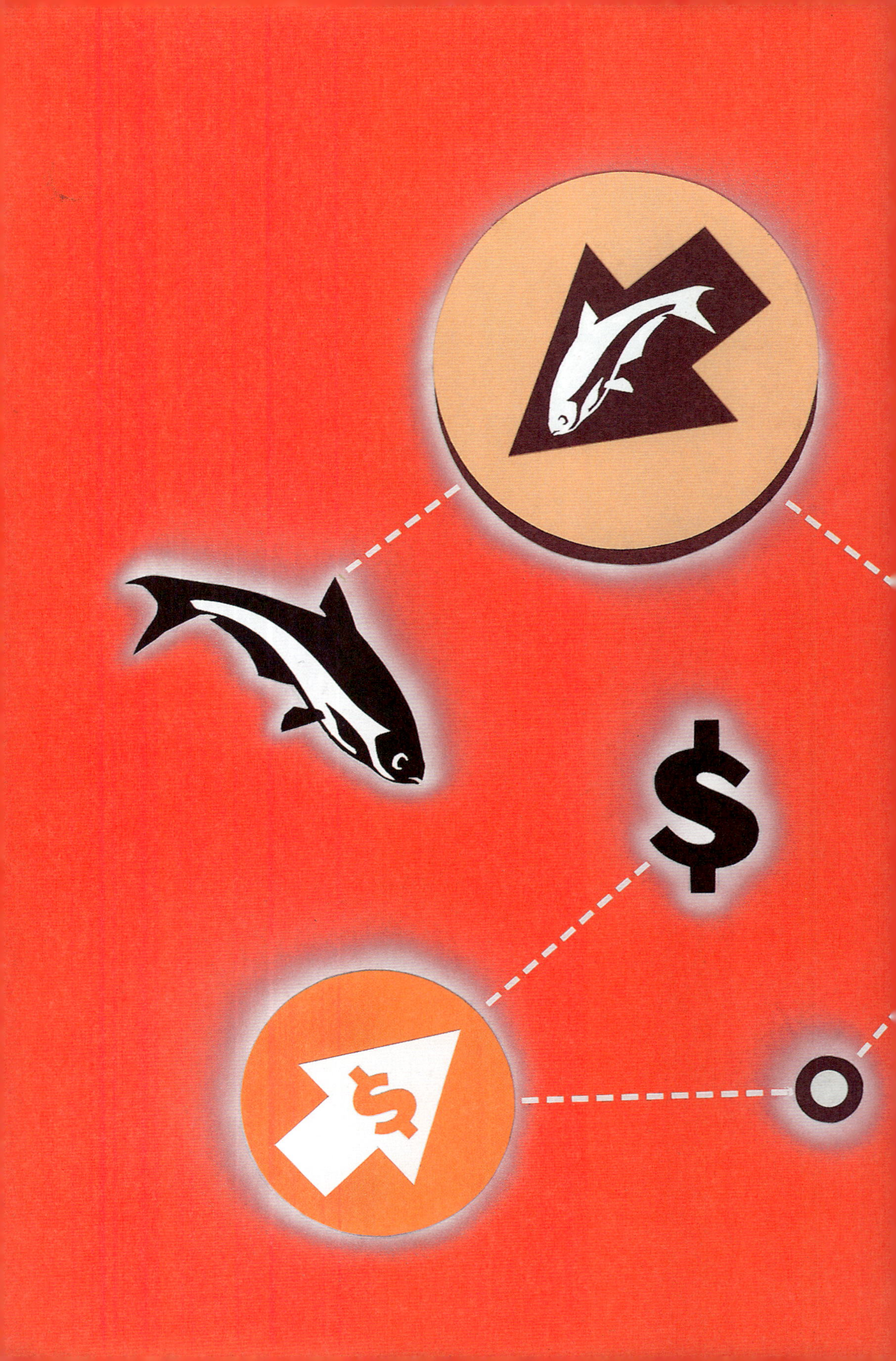

SPECIFIC
APPLICATIONS

The specific business functions described in this chapter illustrate the possibilities and results of Electronic Commerce in more concrete terms. Here, specific sectors and regions have been experimenting with electronic information dissemination and distribution possibilities based on existing SME support networks as well as those being opened up by the Internet.

The chance to go beyond geographic or sectorial restrictions are illustrated and encouraged by way of advanced and user-specific applications, databases, and order systems. From electronic marketing to payment systems, the possibility of enhancing regional and local integration for isolated or less developed areas whilst also providing a window into the international marketplace, are illustrated and refined through these specific initiatives.

Name

ELPRO - Electronic Procurement for Europe

Objectives

To explore requirements and develop a demonstrator system for public procurement that will enable Public Authorities to develop and manage contracts for goods, works and services covered by the procurement directives of the CEC.

Target Group

Public authorities and suppliers

Approach

Development of a demonstrator system by collaborative research and development

Description

The ELPRO system covers the full lifecycle of public procurement and offers help and guidance as to the regulations covering contracts issued and required falling under the procurement directives. The demonstrator is currently being piloted in many organizations across Europe

Schedule

Start date January 1996

Finish June 1999

Countries

UK, Germany, Denmark, Spain, Portugal, Austria

Results

The system devised has been trialled in 4 European countries and is currently being piloted in many organizations. Several reports detailing issues surrounding public procurement have been issued

Future developments

Plans for a commercial system are currently being developed in Austria, UK and Germany. Testing of the effectiveness of such systems will form part of the on-going work after the research project has formally ended. It is planned to continue piloting the system after the conclusion of the research project to assist in developing targetted proposals under the fifth framework programme

Partners

University of Sunderland, UK - Lead partner; City of Newcastle - UK; North Tyneside Council - UK; EDP - Portugal; Telefonica - Spain; Fraunhofer Gesellschaft - Germany; Information Management GmbH - Germany; University of Stuttgart - Germany; Finance Ministry - Austria; Austrian State Printing Office - Austria; Aarhus City Kommune - Denmark; Language Line - UK

Budget

Total project costs approximately 3MECU

Contact details

Centre for Electronic Commerce, University of Sunderland
Andrew Slade

Tel	44 191 5152794
Fax	44 191 5152257
E-mail	andrew.slade@sunderland.ac.uk
URL	http://www.cec.sunderland.ac.uk

Name

PETER - Pilot for Electronic Marketing and Trading in European Small and Medium Enterprises

Objectives

- To demonstrate how European SMEs - sellers and customers - can benefit from the introduction of electronic marketing and trading facilities, saving time, money and resources of work and material.
- To address all aspects of commerce, including advertising, ordering and payment, involving ISDN and the Internet.

Target group

SMEs which trade digital products that need copyright protection. The industrial sectors represented by the partners are basically the information technology, business and management consultancy and multimedia productions. Therefore, the products traded in PETER will basically consist of software solutions, training courseware, multimedia content and consultancy documents.

Approach

PETER aims to address the individual and specific needs of SMEs in different industrial sectors by making use of today's technologies and building on today's networks. For this, 24 SMEs participate in PETER as users. First, they are introduced to e-commerce and IPR issues, then their specific requirements for IPR sensitive e-commerce will be determined. Together with a market analysis, this leads to the specification and implementation of the PETER Pilot. The partners will integrate their respective products into the electronic commerce process of PETER, and three of them will also act as customers. The SMEs will be customers of the respective partners, and may represent all possible kinds of industry.

Description

The project will set up a pilot to demonstrate how European SMEs - sellers and customers - can benefit from the introduction of electronic marketing and trading facilities, saving time, money and resources of work and material. It will be unique in that all aspects of commerce will be addressed, including advertising, ordering and payment, involving ISDN and the Internet.

Schedule

1 November 1997 - 31 October 1999

Countries

Germany, UK, Portugal, France, Belgium, The Netherlands

Results

- An e-commerce online shop validated by the SMEs and customized to their needs during a one year trial
- Training Courseware on Electronic Commerce and related IPR issues

Future developments

- Enhancements of PETER Pilot, continuous adaptation to the needs of the 24 (and other) SMEs.
- Enhancements of the training courseware.

Partners

Teles AG, Berlin (D): coordinator

ALCS, London (GB), Agesfal, Estoril (P), Sincrotel, Estoril (P), CCS, Brussels (B), KCT, Leeuwarden (NL)

Budget

1 MECU (funding: 0,5 MECU)

Contact details

Jens Koblin
TELES AG
Dovestr. 2-4
D-10587 Berlin
Germany

Tel 49.30.39928243
Fax 49.30.3992801
E-mail koblin@teles.de
URL http://www.teles.de

Name

FIWG - Financial Issues Working Group

Objectives

The main purpose of FIWG is to stimulate the deployment of innovative payment systems and transactions mechanisms, such as electronic purse, Internet banking, or micropayments necessary for the development of electronic commerce within the European Union.

Working within the context of the IT Programme of G8 Global Information Society Initiative particularly G8-10 Project of the European Commission, the goal of FIWG is to:

- provide the focal point for exchange and experiences and the discussion of key issues between different parties involved in, or concerned by financial aspects of electronic commerce (banks, technology suppliers, regulatory authorities);
- to play an active role in the promotion and implementation of test beds and pilot projects in the area of electronic payment systems and transaction mechanisms;
- to highlight key issues which are critical to the development of financial infrastructure for electronic commerce;
- to formulate recommendations concerning possible approaches to solving these issues;
- to cooperate with similar groups in the USA and Japan.

Target group

FIWG participants comprises representatives of financial institutions, service organizations, technology suppliers (smart card manufacturers, telecommunications companies, etc) and public authorities (European Commission, European Monetary Institute, etc.)

FIWG aims to establish an industry supported interest group on the subject

Contact details

Mr. Charles Goldfinger	Tel	32 2 7631270
GEF	Fax	32 2 7630947
412 av. de Tervueren	E-mail	chgo.fiwg@www.ispo.cec.be
B- 1150 Brussels	URL	www.businessmedia.net/emb/
Belgium		

TRAINING & RESEARCH

Awareness of Electronic Commerce in general, and Internet skill development in particular, still need to be increased and integrated in the commercial context.
To this end, there is a wide variety of training and research initiatives designed to enhance basic, individual skills as well as allowing the necessary changes to SMEs' current business infrastructures. Here, national and local government, research institutions and business networks are crucial to ensuring the effective and widespread use and application of Electronic Commerce.

The initiatives described in this chapter originate from all the above sources, either separately or in collaboration. Problem areas such as transaction security, competing technical operating standards, and linguistic and cultural barriers to Electronic Commerce use have been both researched and countered by way of tailor-made training programmes and multi-language software. They focus on the transfer of know-how both within and between regions as well as to those SMEs still unaware of Electronic Commerce. The emphasis is on developing 'best practices' and coherent standards - both technically and commercially.

Name

AGORA

Objectives

Establish integrated and tailor-made Electronic Commerce support for Small and Medium-sized organizations

Approach

- Pilot Project based on the One-Stop-Shop concept i.e. provides integrated information, consultancy, and training services through direct access and intermediary organizations.
- Intermediary services are on three levels:
  1. Local One-Stop-Shops (OSS)
  2. Regional Support Units (RSUs) to liaise and cooperate at regional level
  3. European - coordination and supply of particular resources and skills e.g. copyrights, specialized expertise

Description

The One-Stop-Shop concept provides a single point of access to a broad range of business information, training, advice services at the local level and so takes a proactive approach to local needs and conditions. The AGORA Network comprises over 100 OSSs across 25 European regions, expected to increase in the coming year.

Schedule

Start: 01/01/96

End: 31/12/99

Countries

France

UK

Greece

Future developments

By project's end:

- Become self-sustaining
- 50,000 end-users generating an income of 3M ECU per annum
- 50 official AGORA Regional Service Units (run by regional SMC service organizations)
- 250 local service organizations as official AGORA One-Stop-Shops which pay a franchising fee for network services
- 100 consultants, experts, professionals
- 50 multimedia publishers
- 50 on-line service providers and/or Telecom operators generating income of 1m ECU per annum in payment for AGORA support services

Partners

BBC Education, London, UK

Dialogos Nea Media, Athens, Greece

Contact details

Gerard Courtieux

AGORA Project Coordinator

38 Rue Copernic

F 75116 Paris

France

Tel	33 1 53 640192
Fax	33 1 45 021512
E-mail	gerard.SIL@agora.org
URL	http://www.agora.org.uk

Name

Busy City

Objectives

Provide a web-based environment for distance learning of e-commerce

Target Group

University Colleges, SMEs and Public Administrations with programmes to increase competence in modern business informatics in general and electronic commerce in particular

Approach

- Courseware design, production and distribution
- Workshops and collaboration to foster the art of business creation
- Networking in a virtual community for authoring, tutoring and dissemination

Description

A consortium of partners from Sweden, Denmark and United Kingdom have established a virtual city as a web site to provide a learning environment for courses in Electronic Commerce and related fields.

Schedule

Started 1 November 1997

Ends 31 December 1999

Countries

Sweden, Denmark, United Kingdom

Results

Courseware for distance learning in Electronic Commerce adaptable for different target groups

Future developments

Creation of new virtual business companies located in Busy City with products and services accessible through electronic commerce procedures

Contact details

Busy City Conversity AB,
Dr Erik Wallin
Spårsnögatan 14
SE-226 52 Lund, Sweden

E-mail ew@conversity.se
URL http://www.conversity.com

Name

BUSINES LINC

Objectives

- Development of rich Business Innovation Cases
- Establishment of sustainable business innovation services
- Contribution to a future Global Masters Program in EC

Target Group

Managers from enterprises (with special focus on SMEs), students in higher education, executive education

Approach

Development and dissemination of interactive and interlinked case studies

Description

The project develops interactive multimedia cases covering innovative business solutions in the area of electronic commerce and advanced use of IT. Cases will be based on successful real-life situations found in leading enterprises, will show best practices applied, and explain the change process.

Schedule

1 April 98 - 31 March 2000 (duration: 24 months)

Results

18 multimedia case studies in the field of Electronic Commerce (on CD-ROM) and additional online services.

Future developments

Busines-Linc's services will be commercialized after the end of the project.

Partners

University of Cologne (D, coordinator), Copenhagen Business School (DK) Norwegian School of Economics and Business Administration (N), Erasmus University, Rotterdam School of Management (NL), Bocconi University, SDA (Milan, I), Stockholm School of Economics (S)

Contact details

Prof. Dietrich Seibt	Tel	49 221 4705325
University of Cologne	Fax	49 221 4705383
Köln, Germany	E-mail	seibt@wi-im.uni-koeln.de
	URL	www.wi-im.uni-koeln.de/b-linc

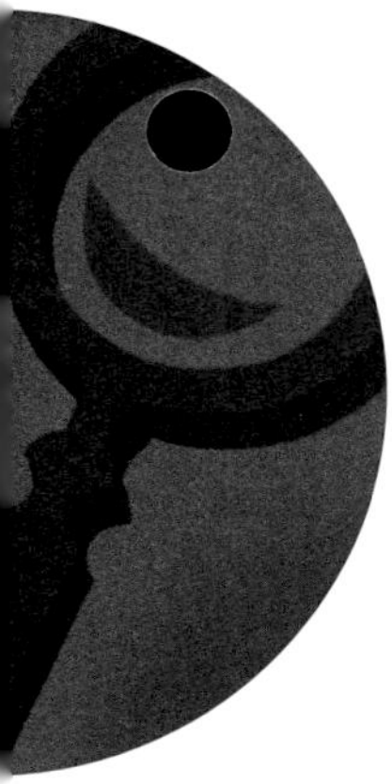

Name

DEUS

Objectives

Collect information and experience about the use of the latest business communications technology provided on the Internet.

Target group

European enterprises

Approach

Empirical research programme, pilot phase.

Description

The first phase of the programme consisted of testing the methodology of the study. The emphasis of the methodology was to offer a series of on-line services and to identify which services should be added, removed or changed.

The final result of the programme was the creation of a fully tested methodology for studying how enterprises have learned to conduct some business processes on-line. The study identified which business processes were conducted efficiently on-line and how enterprises could be supported to implement the new technologies and applications.

Countries

France, Germany, Italy, Spain, The Netherlands, United Kingdom

Results

More than half of the enterprises had no previous experience and were keen on exploiting the technology. The range and nature of the support offered to enterprises made a difference in their acceptance of the technology.
A commitment to change business processes to exploit a presence on the Internet was a common factor for success.

At the end of the pilot the majority of the enterprises expressed the wish to try electronic trading over the Internet in the near future. The majority of the participating enterprises adopted the use of the Internet.

The result of the programme was the creation of a network of expertise and a community of interest: the DEUS club

Partners

- Chambers of Commerce in Amsterdam, Frankfurt, London, Madrid, Milan, Paris
- European Multimedia Forum

Contact details

General Secretariat:
European Multimedia Forum
Rue du Moniteur 9
1000 Brussels
Belgium

Tel	32 2 219 03 05
Fax	32 2 219 32 15
E-mail	secretariat@emf.be
URL	Http://www.deus.org

Name

KISMET - Knowledge of the Information Society for SMEs and Electronic Trade

Objectives

This project addresses the need for content - the identification and development of materials which can be used with SMEs for both the awareness and access stages of this engagement model. These materials will be generic and transferable, able to be adapted to local linguistic, cultural and business environments. They will include demonstrations of actual applications of electronic commerce, and case studies identifying real business benefits, model approaches to identifying business needs and informatics solutions, and options for delivery of awareness and support services to SMEs.

Target Group

- Development bodies (local, regional and national) working with constituencies of SMEs and looking to establish or further develop effective Information Society awareness programmes
- Business developers and intermediaries, including business counsellors and consultants
- SMEs themselves as direct consumers
- Services of the Commission, including DGs III, XIII and XXIII

Approach

The project work plan has been devised as a series of work packages to maximize effective collaborative transnational working within the project and ensure delivery on time and to objectives. The approach to the project recognizes its nature as a dissemination and awareness action.

The key approach to dissemination is the concept of the virtual centre of competence. This provides an added value dissemination network for the results of the project, while at the same time providing much of the content in terms of existing materials and competences.

Description

Provides a network and content supporting the development of Information Society awareness initiatives for SMEs through the Virtual Centre of Competence

Schedule

Start date 1 June 1998 for 12 Months

Countries

UK, Sweden, Denmark, Greece, Netherlands, Italy

Results

Results will include:

- Directory of promoters and initiatives Criteria for assessment and guidelines for development of materials and programmes
- Output which will be both paper based and on line
- Identifying within each member State whether there exists a step by step programme for the introduction of electronic commerce into SMEs
- A model for designing and delivering such programmes
- Importing existing materials from partners and other electronic commerce projects into kismet
- Mechanism to roll out results of all ESPRIT e-commerce projects to SMEs

Future developments

- Through provision of an umbrella (the Virtual Centre of Competence), create a network enabling the location by SMEs and intermediaries of relevant expertise throughout Europe
- Provide a mechanism for the exchange of experience and best practice, between organizations, SMEs, kismet partners, member State government departments and agencies, and other Electronic Commerce projects
- Disseminate existing materials to promoters and SMEs; these materials may be paper based, on line, or demonstration, facilitating the promotion of electronic commerce and its adoption be SMEs
- Develop an inventory of transferable materials and undertake a qualitative analysis and assessment
- Establish an archive of SME case studies demonstrating quantifiable business benefits arising from electronic commerce
- Disseminate the results of European Commission R & D and other ED funded electronic commerce projects to a wider SME audience

Partners

County Durham On-Line (UK), Danish EDI Council (Denmark), EDIFORUM (The Netherlands), Hellenic Electronic Trading Network (Greece), Swedish TelePedagogic Knowledge Centre or (STPKC - Sweden), UnionCamere Dell'Emilia Romagna (Italy)

Contact details

Co Durham On Line
Paul Baker or Clive Smithers
Tel 44 191 383 5001

E-mail Paul.Baker@cdtec.co.uk or Clive.Smithers@cdtec.co.uk
URL http://www.kismet.org.uk

Name

North West Technology Web

Objectives

To provide Innovation and Technology Support Services to SMEs in the North West Of England through traditional and electronic media. Core services : electronic commerce, product and process innovation and technology transfer

Target group

SMEs

Approach

Currently eight Technology Management Centres based at various locations around NW, delivering core services and developing specialisms in innovation and technology support services
3 levels of assistance:

- Awareness through workshops, seminars, exhibitions etc.
- Auditing of company requirements
- Develop in-depth programme of work with company over period of time

Description

Delivery of expert support services in a wide range of activity. Supply chain management programmes, technology transfer, e-commerce activities, business telematics

Schedule

Start date 1 January 1996 through 31 December 1998, with confirmed continuation

Countries

UK based at present

Results

Techweb initially started out as six TMCs in Preston, Blackburn, Skelmersdale, Manchester, Bolton/Bury and Oldham. Increased to eight in 1998 with Halton/Daresbury and Accrington (East Lancs) coming on line. With new funding stream secured, Techweb will expand in size to include Cumbria (Furness) , Liverpool, Wigan, Blackpool and Stockport - thus offering wider geographical base and wider service specialisms

Partners

Techweb is a partnership of over 35 organizations, public and private sector. Including Enterprise plc, local authorities, HEIs and FE colleges, and large private sector partners including British Aerospace, ICL, Royal Mail, IBM, Compaq-Digital, Cooperative Bank, BBC and many others.

Contact details

Karen Preece
NWTW Development Manager
Enterprise plc
17 Ribblesdale Place
Preston
Lancs PR1 3NA

Tel	44 1772 203020
Fax	44 1772 887110
E-mail	preece.k@enterprise.plc.uk
URL	http://www.techweb.co.uk

Name

EUMEDNET - Euro-Mediterranean Network

Objectives

- Promote mutual cooperation and commercial use of the Internet among European and Mediterranean countries.
- Help Mediterranean SMEs to overcome barriers to e-commerce.

Target group

SMEs in Europe and the Mediterranean countries

Approach

- Research & Development on problems of setting up virtual business for SMEs
- Training courses: Internet marketing, electronic payment, legal issues
- Awareness campaigns

Description

EUMEDNET is a consortium of private and academic teams promoting e-commerce for SMEs. It seeks to collaborate with others in facilitating the commercial use of the Internet in Europe and, in particular, Mediterranean countries where linguistic, legal, cultural, technological and economic barriers are hindering Internet use. These barriers put SMEs at a disadvantage in relation to their North American counterparts. Improving and deepening Euro-Mediterranean cooperation is seen as mutually beneficial in this regard.

Schedule

Begun in 1994 and designed to cover a wide range of related fields

Countries

Based in Malaga, Andalucia, Spain, we work closely with teams in Greece, Italy, France, United Kingdom, Finland, Morocco, Tunisia, Egypt, Palestine, Israel, Turkey, Romania, Bulgaria, Slovenia, Malta

Results

- The OBEC'97 Week (Overcoming Barriers to Electronic Commerce) was attended by over 5000 visitors
- The CEPA project (Comercio Electronico en las PYMEs Andaluzas) helped 30 SMEs to set their e-business
- The FEM (Federated Export Marketing) project is helping several SMEs in the building industry.

Future developments

The EUMEDNET project will cover

- Training Business in EC tools
- International Trade, EU Communications & Commercial law
- Information on Internet protocols, programs, interactive multimedia services etc.
- Telematics for Arabic and other Mediterranean languages
- Relevant aspects of Mediterranean economy, culture, commercial uses
- Quality and security issues and systems

Partners

UMA, Universidad de Malaga; ISOCANDA, Andalusian Chapter of ISOC; T2V, Tecnicos en Tiendas Virtuales, S.L.

Budget

Funds from the European Commission, Spanish Government, Junta de Andalucia and private companies.

Please contact

Juan Carlos M. Coll
Facultad de Derecho
Universidad de Málaga
E 29071
Malaga, Spain

Tel	34 95 2229160
Fax	34 95 2132338
E-mail	coll@vnet.es
URL	http://www.eumed.net/ and http://emn.derecho.uma.es/

Name

HELTRANET - Hellenic Electronic Trading Awareness Network

Objectives

- Stimulate cooperation and knowledge exchange between research organizations and business
- Diffuse up-to-date information on latest developments among organizations as well as specific sectors
- Improve national coordination of initiatives by promoting cooperation between Greek regional organizations

Target Group

Greek research and business community

Approach

- Seminars and conferences targeted at specific sectors of the economy
- Major Electronic Commerce events in Greece e.g. conferences
- Production and distribution of information material
- Publication of relevant articles in Greek economics and Information Technology Press
- Participation of HELTRANET members in international conferences e.g. on Electronic Commerce in Greece
- Making opinion leaders in Greek government and business community aware of relevant issues

Description

HELTRANET has been set up to be the focal point for Electronic Commerce awareness and promotion in the Greek scientific and business communities. It is a cooperative venture between Greek universities, public authorities, private companies, vendors and associations, which have an interest in Electronic Commerce. To this end, it is partially funded by the Greek Ministry of Development's General Secretariat for Research and Technology and cooperates with a number of Greek commercial and business associations as well as with the ESPRIT office of the EU DGIII.

Schedule

Underway since January 1996

Countries

Greece

Results

- Five seminars already held and each attended by about 450 participants
- Involved in organization of four major conferences, attended by over 1400 representatives
- Articles published on themes such as Electronic Banking, Electronic Data Exchange (EDI), Financial EDI, Efficient Consumer Response
- HELTRANET members have presented papers at seven international Electronic Commerce conferences in Europe and the USA

Partners

- 14 founding partners
- 29 associated partners
- Prime Contractor is the Research Centre of the Athens University of Economics and Business
- Detailed list of partners available from the Web site

Budget

Partially funded by the Greek General Secretarial of Research & Technology and the various awareness activities

Contact details

Prof. G. Doukidis
Athens University of Economics and Business
76 Patision Str
104 34 Athens
Greece

Tel	30 1 8203160
Fax	30 1 8203183
E-mail	gjd@aueb.gr
URL	http://heltrun.aueb.gr

Name

MediaMit - Neue medien für den Mittelstand

Objectives

Foster rapid uptake of Electronic Commerce by:

- Increasing awareness of electronic transactions
- Customizing and simplifying information and training

Target Group

SMEs - particularly those not yet using Electronic Commerce

Approach

MediaMit is based around the German network for 83 Chambers of Commerce and Industry. It is a tailor-made holistic approach which comprises:

- 'Networks of Excellence' based cooperation between regional, local and national partners (see below) - emphasis is on using existing support networks to gain access to SMEs and to facilitate contact with Electronic Commerce providers and services.
- Best Practice orientated workshops e.g. teleworking, EDI, security issues, on-line services and databases - focus is on step-by-step training.
- exhibitions - knowledge and feedback exchange and also support in developing a common platform for SMEs.

Description

The MediaMit initiative comes under the auspices of the Association of German Chambers of Commerce and Industry (DIHT) which is particularly interested in supporting concentrated, nation-wide initiatives in the field of Electronic Commerce technologies. To this end, it is a core element in organizing events as well as being active in setting up legal and certification frameworks. MediaMit is based on end-user needs, hence continually adapting concepts to changes in new technologies is an important aspect to ensuring customized and accessible information, demonstrations and training.

Schedule

- DIHT has been focusing on multimedia activities in Germany since 1995
- February 1997 - a major MediMit held in Cologne alongside smaller user days at the regional level.

Countries

Germany

Results

- Cologne MediaMit attracted over 500 participants.
- Success of events clearly depends on using a network of experienced and heterogeneous partners in order to ensure diversity e.g. working closely with regional technology industry and regional chambers of industry to ensure a close link between local and national levels of activities.
- Key point for ensuring SME participation and satisfaction by using the trust and experience that exists between SMEs and regional support networks.

Future developments

- Set-up of a permanent Certification Authority (CA)
- Next MediaMit: 12 Feb. 1998, Dortmund Chamber of Industry and Commerce
- Establish Electronic Commerce Competence Centres (e.g. FTK/media NRW)

Partners

- DIHT - Association of German Chambers of Industry and Commerce.
- Regional chambers of Industry and Commerce, local development agencies e.g. Media NRW, and Information Society initiatives.
- Sectorial organizations e.g. trade, insurance, banking, information technology service providers and related small companies.
- National and local media.

Budget

No federal funding necessary as MediaMit partners provide all the funding for any event. Large companies sponsor MediMit at the national level whilst local sponsors in the Electronic Commerce industry provide support at a regional level

Contact details

Bernd Marenbach
DIHT
Adenauerallee 148
53113 Bonn
Germany

Tel	49 228 104606
Fax	49 228 104699
E-mail	bmarenb@bonn.diht.ihk.de
URL	http//www.mediamit.de
	http://www.ihk.de

Name

Transmete-Telematics

Objectives

- Increase the awareness of enterprises on telematics applications and services
- Motivate the introduction of telematics in operational day-to-day activities
- Provide a fundamental understanding of the benefits and of the procedures to be followed for the successful integration and use of these technologies

Target group

- Small and medium size enterprises
- Medium and high level managers
- Business professionals wishing to expand their market share
- Individuals and business consultants wanting to investigate business opportunities on the Internet
- Associations, Chambers and organizations supporting SMEs, wishing to provide value-added services to SMEs.

Approach

Training programme in the form of seminars, workshops, information days, using the following training material:

- Printed material
- Demonstrations on the Internet
- Case studies
- CD-ROM
- Business game to gain experience

Description

The training programme gives an introduction to Telematics, Internet and EDI, with a focus on business activities. Furthermore, the training programme addresses the following issues:

- Required steps to access the market, with a view to the competitors.
- Preparations needed to adapt products to the electronic market.
- Link business activities to a Web site.
- Find partners and to cooperate with them.
- Search for information on sites of the Internet, join discussion groups and mailing lists.
- Product selling and money transactions over the Internet.

Schedule

The project has been completed. The training programme continues.

Countries

Finland, Spain, Greece, Sweden

Results

130 enterprises attended the workshops, 80 more attended the information days and 360 persons attended the seminars (per October 1, 1997). Approx. 6000 SMEs have been reached and have received information and material about the project. The main conclusion from the project is that SMEs require consultancy and case-specific assistance in order to introduce innovation in their day-to-day activities.

Future developments

- Tailor-made seminars for one enterprise at a time
- Sector-specific seminars to address the same sector

Partners

Kemi Tornio Polytechnic, Finland
Oulu Institute of Technology, Finland
Eurocom Expertise, Greece
Hellenic Esprit Club, Greece
Planet S.A., Greece
Carsa S.A., Spain
Institut Catala de Telematica Aplicada S.A., Spain
Nextel S.A., Spain
Centek, Sweden
Norbotten Chamber of Commerce, Sweden

Contact details

Vassiliki C. Amenta
EUROCOM EXPERTISE S.A.
372, Messogion Ave
15341 Agia Paraskevi
Greece

Tel	30 1 6010409
Fax	30 1 6010405
E-mail	bame@eurocom.gr
URL	http://www.eurocom.gr

Name

The Electronic Commerce and EDI Centre for Wales

Objectives

Provides information, advice and assistance to the Welsh business community on the optimum adoption of EDI and Electronic Commerce

Target Group

Welsh companies and small businesses in particular

Approach

Provides the following services

- Quarterly magazine - printed and online
- Industry seminars designed for specific sectors
- Company workshops on request
- Implementation and Financial support services during pilot phase
- Information service on request or in centre's library

Description

The Centre was established by the European Commission and Welsh Development Agency to provide information, advice and assistance to the Welsh business community to make adopting Electronic Commerce as smooth, cost effective and advantageous as possible. This is being achieved by supporting SMEs in undertaking EDI and EC developments.

Countries

United Kingdom

Partners

The Welsh Centre is part of a European Network of Awareness Centres, which also includes the Scottish EDI Centre and the Electronic Commerce Association.

Contact Details

Michael O'Shea,
EC and EDI Centre for Wales
Welsh Development Agency
Principality House, The Friary
Cardiff, CF1, 4AE
United Kingdom

Tel 44 1222 828703
Fax 44 1222 828806
E-mail edi@edi.wales.org
URL www.edi.wales.org

ANNEXES

Name	**Ad Valorem**
Description	A standing invitation to share a cross-enterprise engagement platform. It challenges prospective users of e-commerce tools/services, and their vendors/providers, to a collaborative search / production of added value.
Country	Italy
Contact details	Pharos Services Italia Sas, Luigi Bertuzzi Tel/Fax 39 051 303727 E-mail bertuzzi@pharos-it.com URL http://www.pharos-it.com

Name	**Centre for Study of Electronic Commerce**
Description	Researches how Electronic Commerce can be used. The center also organizes an annual conference on EC.
Country	Slovenia
Contact details	University of Maribor, Faculty of Organizational Sciences Joze Gricar Tel 386 64 374 291 E-mail gricar@uni-lj.si URL http://ecom.fov.uni-mb.si

Name	**COMPASS - Centre of Multimedia Promotion And Support Services for Textile & Clothing-**
Description	COMPASS is developing multimedia services to support the introduction of Textile&Clothing companies into the e-commerce. Development of virtual shops, awareness road-show, development of a Textile Trade Center based on Internet, a purchase centre and a virtual fair are some of these services.
Country	Spain
Contact details	CETEMMSA Mr Carles Fradera / Mrs Montse Morón Tel 34 93 7419100 Email cetemmsa@cetemmsa.es URL http://www.cetemmsa.es

Name	**Connect**
Description	The Internet centre for Merseyside businesses: raising awareness and providing training and facilities for local organizations to conduct commerce over the Internet.
Contact details	Connect, University of Liverpool Bernard Friery Tel 44 151 7948273 E-mail bernie@connect.org.uk URL http://www.connect.org.uk/

Name	**e-Christmas**
Description	The e-Christmas project centers around the creation and operation of an innovative multi-lingual, multi-currency retail Web site which will market Christmas gifts from retailers and manufacturers in nine European countries to Internet consumers around the world
Country	France, Germany, Ireland, Italy, Netherlands, Norway, Spain, Switzerland, UK
Contact details	IMRG James Roper Tel 44 171 3036603 E-mail James@imrg.org URL http://www.e-Christmas.com/

Name	**EDI Business Austria**
Description	Promotion of the use of Electronic Commerce and EDI through awareness and training activities, free initial consultation, realization and support.
Country	Austria
Contact details	ITF Programm Management für EDI Herbert E. Thomas Tel 43 2266 71689 E-mail thomas@edi.at URL http://www.edi.at

Name **E-LAB - Comercio Electronico Global**

Description Comercio Electronico Global has set up a laboratory (E-LAB) for the development of pilot tests, experiments, product and service efficiency tests, as well as for presenting ecommerce systems, business operation models, etc. to SMEs and universities. All these activities are conducted from an impartial point of view.

Country Spain

Contact details Comercio Electronico Global
Eduardo Paz Lloveras
Tel 34 976 358491
E-mail eduardopaz@technologist.com
URL www.geocities.com/CapeCanaveral/Lab/9964/

Name **Electronic Commerce Education CD-ROM**

Description The CD-ROM provides information on various possibilities of Electronic Commerce in the form of Computer Based Training, combined with on-line lectures. The current CD-ROM is in German, an English version is planned.

Country Germany

Contact details Saxony Telematics Development Corporation
Ulf Schmidt
Tel 49 341 14793693
Fax 49 341 9927909
E-mail set4@set.saxony.de

Name **ERIM Centre for Electronic Commerce**

Description Business cases for Electronic Commerce in SMEs. Supply Chain Engineering.

Country USA

Contact details Center for Electronic Commerce
Steve Harris
Tel 1 734 669-8007 x 3570
E-mail cecinfo@erim.org
URL http://www.erim.org

Name **EURIM**

Description A Web site providing information compiled by an all-party, parliament-industry group concerned with Informatics and Telematics. The Web site covers Electronic Commerce, Telecom, Internet, Standards strategy, Smart cards, et al.

Country United Kingdom

Contact details	Telecommunications Managers Association David Harrington Tel 44 1372 361234 E-mail dg@tms.org.uk URL http://www.tma.org.uk/ecom

Name	**Global Market for SMEs**
Description	First stop web site for global e-commerce market for SMEs, building on the G8 pilot project conferences/exhibitions in UK in 1998..
Country	UK
Contact details	Cequel Plus Ltd Anthony Seaberg Tel 44 171 931 7766 Email anthony@cequel.co.uk URL www.globalmarket.org.uk

Name	**HELTRUN**
Description	Research, development and training group for Electronic Commerce in Athens University of Economics and Business
Country	Greece
Contact details	William Drakos Tel 30 1 8203154 E-mail asd@aueb.gr URL http://heltrun.aueb.gr

Name	**Impresa Monitor**
Description	A telematic dialogue among SMEs in the Rome region aimed at providing E-mail communication facilities to exchange product information.The project also includes the creation of an electronic catalogue of SMEs/products.
Country	Italy
Contact details	Promoroma Ms Flavia d'Auria Tel 39 6 6795941 E-mail promoroma@mclink.it URL http://www.promoroma.com

Name	**Manchester Technology Management Centre**
Description	The centre assists companies to identify, develop and commercialize new products, process and technologies that meet market needs.
Country	England
Contact details	Luqman Hayes
	Tel 0161 908 0523
	E-mail luqman.hayes@mtmc.org.uk
	URL http://www.mtmc.org.uk

Name	**MIDAS-NET**
Description	MIDAS-NET is an initiative of the INFO2000 programme which is aimed at stimulating interest, demonstrating new products in the multimedia market, and assisting information users to exploit the potential of multimedia content.
Country	Austria
Contact details	Austrian Federal Economic Chamber - Foreign Trade Department
	Günther Lechner
	Christian Rupp
	Tel 43 1 50105 4556
	E- mail lechnerg@aw.wk.or.at and ruppc@aw.wk.or.at
	URL http://www.midas.at

Name	**Modern Communication Tools for SMEs**
Description	Seminars and road show aimed at increasing awareness of Electronic Commerce among SMEs.
Country	Poland
Contact details	Polish SME Foundation, Tomasz Klimczak
	Tel 48 22 6997044 or 48 22 6997045
	E-mail zarzad@msp.org.pl
	URL http://www.msp.org.pl

Name	**Network Commerce**
Description	Creating integrated learning environments for developing technological and business skills, and "key" qualities required in the virtual marketplace.
Country	Ireland
Contact details	City of Galway Vocational Education Committee, Jim Brick
	Tel 353 91 567194
	E-mail jim.brick@cgvec.ie

Name	**Pentagon Project - Information Society Initiative**
Description	PENTAGON delivers the DTI's ISI programme in the North East of England. Activities include awareness raising, themed workshops, support for business consultancy and project implementation.
Country	North East region of UK covering Durham, Northumberland, Sunderland, Tees Valley and Tyneside
Contact details	Co Durham On Line Paul Baker or Clive Smithers Tel 44 191 383 5001 E-mail Paul.Baker@cdtec.co.uk or Clive.Smithers@cdtec.co.uk URL http://www.pentagon.ne-isi.co.uk URL http://www.cdol.co.uk

Name	**SME-WEB**
Description	SME-WEB is a service for the European small and medium sized enterprises. It gives the possibility of going through Austrian, Italian and EC data bases where advice and information on the management, the market and the financing of enterprises can be found.
Country	Austria
Contact details	Austrian Federal Economic Chamber - Foreign Trade Department Guenther Lechner Christian Rupp Tel 43 1 50105 4556 E- mails lechnerg@aw.wk.or.at and ruppc@aw.wk.or.at URL http://www.wk.or.at/sme-web

Name	**Telerise**
Description	An independent knowledge and technology transfer organization helping companies integrate on-line business technology. Visit the web-site for case-studies, updates and an SME-focused information resource.
Country	United Kingdom
Contact details	Telerise Chris Sullivan Tel 44 114 2228280 E-mail telerise@sheffield.ac.uk URL http://www.telerise.shef.ac.uk

Name	**TIEKE, Finnish Information Technology Development Centre**
Description	One of TIEKEs main functions is to promote Electronic Commerce. TIEKE takes part in developing industry specific solutions that help SMEs to adopt EC e.g. in the textile and clothing, furniture and food industry.
Countries	**Finland**
Contact details	TIEKE, Aatto J. Repo Salomonkatu 17 A 10 th floor FIN-00100 Helsinki, Finland Tel 358 9 47630350 Fax 358 9 47630399 Email aatto.j.repo@tieke.fi URL http://www.tieke.fi/

Name	**TMA**
Description	An independent user organization providing its members (senior telecom and info system managers in the business sector) with professional services and information. Increasingly, TMA's focus is on e-commerce
Country	United Kingdom
Contact details	David Harrington (Director General) Tel 44 1372 361234 E-mail dg@tma.org.uk URL http://www.tma.org.uk URL http://www.tma-online.com

Annex B *Index of initiatives by country*

Annex C *Alphabetical index & relevant Web sites*